Riding Past Grief:
A Daughter's Journey

By
Deborah Rebeck Ash

Proctor Publications, LLC
P.O. Box 2498
Ann Arbor, Michigan, 48106
(800) 343-3034
www.proctorpublications.com

Printed in the United States of America

Publisher's Cataloging-in-Publication
(Provided by Quality Books)

Ash, Deborah Rebeck.
    Riding past grief : a daughter's journey / by
Deborah Rebeck Ash. -- 1st ed.
    p. cm.
    LCCN: 00-130333
    ISBN: 1-882792-92-0

    1. Grief--Poetry. 2. Mothers--Death--Poetry.
3. Mothers and daughters--Poetry.   I. Title.

PS3551.S336R54 2000   811'.6
                    QBI00-226

Proctor Publications, LLC • Ann Arbor • Michigan • USA

When My Heart Stops

When my heart stops I shall be far away from this place.
My soul will soar upon new currents, unattainable before.
There will be no need for tears or pain, just joy, sheer joy,
      joy with the wind lifting my soul beyond every barrier.
My heart will get rest when it stops in this world,
      rest from continual demands and duress.
No need to pump life to a renewed spirit soaring
      by the touch of God's mercy and unfailing love.
When it stops, my heart broken, out will spill diamonds,
      life-jewels carefully polished in the crucible of me.
Diamonds for all, sparkling and free
      catching the sun in countless facets of delight.
When my heart stops my work will be done.
I'll be free in God's wind, empowered by His love
      while earthly life trudges on and on and on
      using up time in its customary way.
My heart beats faithfully 'til then, a temporary power source
      incessantly working 'til released by God's light
      asking no fee for its constant toil,
      knowing my song will resound forever.

1996

Grief poems in memory of
my mother
Joanne D. Rebeck
born October 11, 1925
died September 26, 1998

Riding Past Grief:
A Daughter's Journey

Each year I write birthday poems for my children. For many years they never knew the poems existed. These were gifts for later. Not until the week of her death had I ever written a poem about my mother. I tried writing during her illness, but nothing would come. After she died, the floodgates of grief were opened and have not yet closed. My poems became a way of grieving, not only for me but for my father as well. He rarely sheds tears but acknowledged he could not read the poems without needing a tissue. He would read them, shed a tear, and we would talk about Mother. These poems have been a cleansing gift and a memorial to an amazing woman. What is even more surprising is how prolific I was while finishing work on a doctorate in flute performance at the University of Michigan.

Here are my grief poems and the inspirations behind them. This collection encompasses one year, beginning with the cancer diagnosis in May 1998 to a year later, May 1999. After much thought, I decided to organize the poems in the order written, enabling the reader to follow my own grief walk.

Work on this project has been grief therapy for us all. Thanks goes to my family for illustrating this volume, to my daughter for her cover artwork, and to my friends who read each poem as it was born. These friends continually supported and encouraged me in my drive to publish this first poetry collection. Photos are from my family album and the unsorted box we tried to have Mother label during her illness. Special thanks goes to Edgar Westrum for photographing the priceless advent dinner theater event at our church and to W. Edward Wendover, publisher of the Plymouth Canton *Community Crier*, one of the finest community papers in the country, for releasing Chris Boyd's photo of my mother and her grandchildren. Finally, I would like to thank my mother for all her support during my lifetime. As an English teacher, Mother passed on to me her passion for words and the craft of writing. She loved reading my poetry and shared my delight in the written word. I miss her enthusiasm and penchant for editing. To her I am greatly indebted.

All but six poems were written after Mother's death. She read only two: *When My Heart Stops* and *Mother-Daughter Walk*. *When My Heart Stops* was written in 1996, a time when Mother was healthy. Death and old age seemed far off. When she read it, my mother instantly requested it to be read at her funeral. Neither of us expected that time to come soon, but I kept my promise, and the poem was read by a good friend. How true my words were. She is free and far away. Her work is done, but her song still resounds in my heart.

Mother-Daughter Walk is my daughter's birthday poem written eight days after Mother's colon surgery and cancer diagnosis. The poem was read aloud at a church mother-daughter luncheon that very afternoon. Our associate pastor read *Mother-Daughter Walk*, and I read several of my earlier poems in what became my first poetry reading and the beginning of my grief journey.

Deborah Rebeck Ash

Riding Past Grief:
A Daughter's Journey

Mother's presence made life rich.

Mother-Daughter Walk

Fifteen years past we walked,
    my mother, you, and I,
    you a babe new, fresh, experiencing.
Still for me time stood.
Tense electric currents of reality
    jolted our peaceful world.
New walks in same surroundings,
    you, my mother, and I,
    pondered the cancer within
    noticing familiar things new
    just as you were
    new, fresh, curious.
Trees seemed closer,
    more colorful and real,
    birds' flight a challenge,
    swiftly soaring, silently freeing.
You were our gift then,
    a mother's wondrous miracle,
    a grandmother's joy of posterity,
    a father's second love.

We survived the threat.
You grew in body and I within.
God's gift, mothering came easy.
You gave new vistas for my narrow perspective.
Humbled by your presence,
    your growth encouraged more in me.
My mother became my friend again
    as you have always been.

We'll walk this mother-daughter
   walk together for awhile.
Richer we become new, fresh,
   repeating with each generation.
Mothers and daughters carry
   part of each other down new walks
   thankful for those who walked ahead.

May 9, 1998

Fifteen years ago my mother successfully battled breast cancer. After awhile, we took each healthy year for granted. With this second diagnosis, I wanted another fifteen or more years for my family.

Cancer Eyes

Cat eyes
  hungry eyes
  caring eyes
  loving eyes
Everyone has eyes
  blue
  brown
  green
  hazel
Then there are cancer eyes
  sunken
  void
  suffering
  window to death.

                                June 22, 1998

It was impossible for me to write during Mother's illness. I came home from my parents' house drained. "Cancer Eyes" captures the hollowness of my mother's eyes after the fourth week of chemotherapy. She did fine until then. It was at this point when I saw death, a chilling reminder of my grandfather's eyes when he was in a nursing home many years ago.

Three Months

Three months left, that's all that I have.
What will I do in the time I have left?
What can I leave for those left behind
    to remember me after three months pass?

Do nothing, I die as my body succumbs
    to the cancer within growing out of control.
I can fight for my life, go beyond hopes,
    live as a miracle, hope in a cure.

With new hope I can live each day as a gift
    giving in turn by the grace I've been given.
Once past, three months grow into years,
    living water, where once had been tears.

What will I do then, with more life to live?
Will I live it the same as I've done all along?
Do nothing, my soul succumbs, won't do.
Forever changed, I'll work for His glory.
                    July 23, 1998

The cancer doubled during treatment. Mother was given three months to live. Of course, she expected to beat it. I had a hard time understanding how Mother was using her time. I would have thrown a party and invited my friends to say "good-bye," but she was determined to live. "Three Months" looks at the situation as if I had three months to live.

Joanne's Closets

Behind closed doors her clothes await,
       neatly hung by season, utility, function.
Many unworn, price tags still cling
       as Christmas ornaments on a virgin tree.
Clothes-filled closets neatly arranged,
       king's concubines awaiting their call,
       fashion's fleeting glory.
Blessed with a body for clothes to grace,
       she shopped and bought, shopped and bought,
       saving for special days that never came.
Now weak from illness,
       cancer chooses the robes she wears
       while silent closets wait
       for an unknown time.
Someday she'll be on the other side.
No princess Di crowds to throng
       to her pregnant closets.
But doors will open.
Free gifts to all
       carefully selected, released
       from Joanne's closets
       for that special day.
Star-kissed, she will be
       in new garments of purest white.
The time is now.

                September 20, 1998

Days before Mother died, I sensed the end was near. I could not understand how anyone could bounce back from where she had been. It seemed I gained every pound she had lost.

Piping Wild

Dying well these
    piping wild cancer days,
    unreachable by laser.
Drugged healing waits
    beyond reviving touch,
    ugly boundary-less disease.

The piper calls,
    rat scavenging ears.
Incessant sounds scratch,
    pierce deadly accuracy,
    sonic destruction complete.
Good dies with bad.

High price dying well,
    eats the soul, robs the heart.
Wild piping increases madness
    reducing to basics.
Well dying steals the living.
Steep cost exterminates all.

September 24, 1998

"Piping Wild" vented my frustration. While Mother was dying, I was also preparing for doctoral oral examinations and an orchestral flute concerto performance of John Corigliano's "Pied Piper Fantasy." I had difficulty focusing until I realized I could eliminate cancer instead of mice with my music. Practicing became a mission. My first rehearsal with the orchestra two days after Mother's death was a challenge. Performing with the Plymouth Symphony Orchestra three weeks later, I felt Mother's presence beyond the spotlights.

Final Moments

Breathe in life
   exhale living
   breathe in family
   exhale love
   breathe in love
   exhale living
   concentrated life
   basic essentials
   breathe in love
   exhale love
   breathe in family
   exhale love
   breathe in
   exhale...
          September 26, 1998

Written the day she died, this poem recreates the last moments in my mother's life. When she stopped talking, we surrounded her bed, held her hands, and told her we loved her. I could feel love in every breath.

I Wear My Mother's Clothes

I wear my mother's clothes,
    the ring she wore, her socks and shoes.
They comfort, surround me
    with her smell, her essence.

I wear my mother's clothes
    as sorrowful daughter.
Though gone from sight,
    I feel her presence, her spirit.

I will wash her clothes soon.
They become mine
    as I walk with memories
    of her in my heart.

                                October 1, 1998

After the memorial service we returned to my parents' house. Still dressed up, I simply went into my mother's closet and picked out an entire new outfit. Right down to the sneakers. I found unexpected comfort wearing her clothes.

4:20

I previewed your death
       in a dream the night before
       when it snowed on July 4
       and no one came for fireworks.
It was 4:20 a.m. when I awoke
       and you were gone.
I shivered in the barren snow.
The bathroom became my refuge.
And then peace came, unexpected
       joy sprang from sorrow.
We drove across snow-filled parking lots,
       empty, void, we were alone.
I threw on extra covers and returned
       to sleep in another world
       where death does not exist.

The day you died I cried,
       held your hand as you left
       this world for another.
You wanted to go, but loved us so,
       breathing in our love.
At 4:20 p.m. you left.
We let you go into angel's wings.
I heard their rustle in your last breath.

Awake again that night, I cried.
Now angelic heralds by your side
       swept up in iridescent purity,
       fireworks over snow-swept fields.

Again, I witnessed your entrance
    to timeless eternity at 4:20 a.m.
You reached from beyond
    soothing my soul with eternal love.
October 4, 1998

"4:20" combines reality with dream. The day she died, I awoke at 4:20 a.m. In a dream, Mother had just died. Shortly thereafter, I felt a tremendous heavenly peace. The next morning, after her death, I again woke at 4:20 a.m. This time I realized the dream had been a premonition of death and eternity.

The Memorial Garden at Westminster Presbyterian Church.

"Dust to Dust" occurred to me during the interment of Mother's cremains. I was not expecting to see ashes float up to the sky. It was comforting to watch her remains become airborne glitter rising heavenward as "diamonds for all."

Dust to Dust

Dust to dust, we become one with the soil.
Mourning family bids adieu
    by the rain-cleansed soil.
Sun shines in the garden
    though our hearts are heavy,
    viewing the hole where she will stay
    mixed with dirt becoming dust in the ground.
Watching gray dusty remains fall down,
    down into the waiting earth,
    my gaze follows a fine golden cloud,
    sunny breeze rising reflections.
Her remains disperse, floating up to the sun.
Peace reflects in each rising particle.
Though earth-bound in body, the spirit soars.
Spirit dust surrounds my soul, lifts my heart.
Dust to dust, we become one in spirit.
We become one forever.
October 5, 1998

Love You For Eternity

You loved me before I was born,
taught me about life,
sheltered me from storms.

Parting from your hospital bed,
desperate with fear,
you whispered in my ear,
Love you for eternity.

I left through crystal tears,
returned to watch you die,
held your hands,
through tears I cried,
watering your grave,
Love you for eternity.

October 6, 1998

"Love You For Eternity" was an expression we shared. It was difficult for me to leave Mother in the hospital while we took our yearly trip to Montana. By then she was getting experimental treatment: two constant weeks of chemotherapy and twice daily doses of radiation. When we visited her in the hospital, she frequently took walks down the corridors with us. This time she walked us to the elevator. As we parted, she hugged me and whispered in my ear, "Love you for eternity." A moment I will never forget.

JOANNE D. REBECK
PEACE IN CHRIST
1925-1998
I LOVE YOU
FOR ETERNITY
CSR SJR DRA JLA
SEH EDA MMA

Joanne's memorial brick at Arbor Hospice, Ann Arbor, Michigan.

Joanne with her daughters, July 1954.

Joanne with her grandchildren, July 1986.

A Mother's Love

I didn't understand your love as I grew.
I just knew it was there, teaching me,
      sometimes smothering, always mothering.
Unbroken love between mother and daughter,
      emblazoned with your initials, voice, style,
      you loved as only you knew.
In the end, aloud, I loved you too.
Not as much as a mother loves
      a daughter, was your vow.
How would you know
      the depth of my love?
At your death I didn't understand
      your love compared to mine.
Feel the depth, know it is there.

Now I understand your love as I weep,
      know you are still here reaching me,
      never smothering, always mothering,
      purified and perfected by grace.
A mother's love reaches beyond the grave,
      umbilical cord between two worlds,
      unbroken love showered from above.
I am comforted by your love,
      know you feel the depth of mine.
Your love transcends all worlds for eternity.

October 6, 1998

"A Mother's Love" was the result of a conversation we had. The day before she died, I told Mother I loved her. She told me it was not as much as she loved me. It was as if we were in a battle of who loved the most. In the end I think she was right, for I continue to feel her love even though she is gone from this world.

I Know Death

I know death,
     looked it in the face,
     opposite birth process,
     natural exit,
     entrance to another world,
     ugly facade for all to fear.
We dread the inevitable
     as if it never comes,
     but it does.
Death wants fear of finality,
     but has no victory.
Doorway to heaven,
     trap-door to hell,
     the real threat is
     heaven or hell.
Death becomes a vehicle
     to our final destination.
I know death is not final.
It is a new beginning.

October 7, 1998

Watching Mother die decreased my fear of death. I discovered it to be a natural life event which, unfortunately, our society puts in a locked closet. Although at the time I wanted my sister to come relieve me so I could go home, I would not change a thing from how it actually occurred. Our time at Hospice helped our family experience and process this natural event in a compassionate way. Death is never non-stressful, but Mother's was peaceful and glorious.

Vibrant Woman

Vibrant woman, loving and giving,
    devoted to family, inspiring all who knew her.
Delightful woman, warm and caring
    in her loving and gracious enthusiasm for living.
Delightful lady, energetic and dedicated,
    touched the lives of scores of people
    with her enthusiasm and joyful spirit.
Vivacious lady, kind and helpful
    with her upbeat cheery attitude--
    lived life to the fullest.
Wonderful woman, beaming with pride--
    vivacity, zest for living.
Remarkable woman, vibrant and accomplished,
    neat, in more ways than one.
Exuberant lady, positive and upbeat,
    enthusiastic, bubbling spirit, special sparkle.
Vital woman, so much to give--
    joyous radiance, sparkling eyes,
    contagious smile, cheerful ways.
Amazing woman, with zest for life--
    vibrant, happy smile, full of vitality.
Vibrant woman, energetic forever.
Peace in God's arms, her vibrance is missed.

October 8, 1998

"Vibrant Woman" grew out of nightly depression. I became extremely depressed around dinner time, a time when I had helped out during Mother's illness. It was devastating. One night, to break the depression, I read through all the sympathy cards I received and made a list of the adjectives people used to describe her. It was amazing how each person captured the same essence: her vitality. The list became this poem.

Joanne reading to her grandchildren.

Starlight

Starlight, star bright,
    first star I see tonight.
Starlight, star bright,
    Joanne's joy is God's delight.
Starlight, star bright,
    I know she fought the good fight.
Starlight, star bright,
    Joanne's star is burning bright.
Starlight, star bright,
    watch my family through the night.
Starlight, star bright,
    to her memories we hold tight.
Starlight, star bright.

October 8, 1998

My mother loved reciting nursery rhymes when I was little. Only when I read them repeatedly to my own young children did I understand how she knew them so well. They are now a part of me.

Joanne and her mother, 1940's.

Joanne and her daughters, 1997.

Mothers and Daughters

Mothers and daughters come in all kinds.
Some are time-delayed mirror images bonded in glue.
Others are opposites, magnetized by heredity.
Best are the kind who share life and care.

Modern distances derail closeness.
Corporate expansion creates a generational loss.
Rare are the days when mothers and daughters stay
    in the same town for generations.

Regardless, the bond travels with each move,
    strongest through daily nurturing.
Mothers and daughters who live nearby
    share ups and downs, good sides and bad.

Daughters and mothers intricately intwined,
    knowing each other's dimensions so well,
    sometimes driving each other nuts by the closeness.
Only when it is gone is it missed.

October 10, 1998

As an only child, Mother always lived near her mother. Living in the same town as my mother caused me to strike a balance between my life and our bond. My sister chose to live in Montana. When she visited, we always packed a lot of living into a short time.

The Way We Die

The way we die
  unlearned, unrehearsed.
We are novices
  on a journey
  with one chance.
It cannot be replayed
  or redone.

October 11, 1998

Mother wanted to die with dignity. A perfectionist to the end, she wanted to do it right. Her brief stay (twenty-one hours) at Arbor Hospice gave her that opportunity.

Phone Call to Heaven

Hello, Lord. Please put me through.
I want to say "Hello" to your newest resident.
Just this once, let her hear my voice.
I know she won't be able to talk
      or carry on a conversation.
I know she's safe in your shelter.
Just let me call her, tell her I love her
      and got her clear message.
I got it alone while driving my car,
        told me she'd arrived right by your side,
        told me I'd a mother in heaven.
Imagine an advocate, all just for me!
Watch out, she's a fireball,
      you know that by now.
To you I feel closer with her as my guide.
Let my call through this time or I'll cry.
It's her birthday, you know, send her our wishes.
The children are growing, missing her joy,
      new things to tell everyday.
But then, she probably already knows.
Put my call through, please put it through.
If not, maybe just this once, please.
Let me record it on voice mail forever.
                October 11, 1998

This was my mother's only birthday poem from me. She missed her birthday by two weeks. Two days after she died, I was driving alone when I really did get a message from her: I had a mother-advocate in heaven. Again, I felt her love beyond the grave.

Big *Let-Go*

Life's one big *let-go*.
I know how it works,
     been on both sides
     as a kid and a mom.
First, let go from the womb,
     childhood, a continual release.
We want to hold and keep.
Life doesn't work that way.
Mothers must continually let go.
Can we let go and love just the same?
Death, the ultimate *let-go,*
     requires leaving all behind.
Those who remain must release
     loved ones to another dimension.
Can't we touch, hold, keep forever?
Touch lets us know we're real.
Holding gives security.
Keeping helps us feel well-armed.
No one ever is ready
     for the final *let-go*.
Funny thing, when you finally do it,
     feel the bond strengthened
     tighter than you could ever hold.
Touch takes on new meaning,
     from textural to spiritual.
Feel secure holding memories
     keeping loved ones close.

The big *let-go* becomes smaller,
    just a stretch between dimensions.
We don't have to let go at the end,
    just open ourselves, extend our reach,
    expand in all dimensions until
    it becomes a big *gathering-in*
    of all that was released.

October 13, 1998

In life my mother was often obsessed with control. Letting go was difficult for her to do. Only at the very end did she succeed.

Fall Colors

Wind whipped branches bend briskly.
Released upon invisible air currents,
    trees weep colorful falling leaves.
Swirls of yellow, crimson, rust, purple,
    airborne colors cascade and fall:
    brilliant yellow, bright hope illuminated,
    fiery sun flaming crimson,
    airborne rust anxiety flipping,
    purple, majestic perfection, peace.
All fall, scattered across the grass,
    soon to be blown away.
Only the skeletal trunk remains,
    foundation keeper for next spring's glory.
Your colors are brilliantly displayed,
    wind released birth through death:
    hope in bright yellow forests,
    crimson passion for living
    marred by tomorrow's worry
    protected by faith painted in purple.
Leaves swirl up, down, around, and fall.
In brilliant display all are dispersed.
Heart memories retain your essence.

October 15, 1998

One autumn morning I savored the sight of our beautiful Purple Ash tree, leaves singly cascading to the ground. I felt a poem in the beauty. Mother always said we usually have a warm spell full of vibrant colors in time for her birthday. She called it, "Indian Summer," for its natural beauty.

Legacy

Rings surround, diamonds glitter,
    things collect dust, clothes wear out,
    silver sparkles and tarnishes, gold gleams,
    photos eventually decay,
    money gets spent, land used,
    but words, once said, resound.
Actions, words, intangible legacy,
    the only things we leave behind
    speak for us when we are gone.
Jewelry worn becomes another's,
    radiance of joy encircles its wearer.
Kindness lifts a soul, gets passed around.
What legacy has passed from you to me?
It is not found in jewel cases or banks.
It surrounds me, shimmering hope.
Your legacy continues in me.
I gather in all that you were
    as butterflies returning to nest.
Far beyond reach they fly to my heart
    with your nectar--joy, hope, energy,
    vibrancy packaged in a neat chrysalis
    waiting for my winter to end.
As jeweled wings flutter against blue sky,
    annual rebirth, renewal, returning home,
    your legacy continues beyond time.

October 16, 1998

During her illness, I often wondered what would be my mother's legacy to me. She did not sew, was an average cook, had drawers full of photos not in albums, but loved to shop. Only when the sympathy cards arrived did I begin to understand. Her vibrant energy was her legacy.

Heart Tears

Though you're gone, I feel your strength as mine wanes.
Grieving squeezes the soul, wringing out heart tears.
Mine runs dry, waiting to be filled again and again.
I find hidden strength, your spirit filling me anew.
God's hot-line connection you've become,
      power source from another world.
Thanks for showing me your strength when I was young,
      displaying gracious hospitality, outgoing giving.
Flaws, part of the package, are burnished in sorrow,
      cleansed pure, washed clean in my tears.
Heart tears flow freely for new tomorrows.

October 16, 1998

I did not expect to feel closeness to my mother after she died. It has been a pleasant surprise to feel her comfort from a direct heavenly connnection, my own personal contact.

Christmas Cactus

This winter past my cactus bloomed
    yielding tender delicate pink flowers.
Never regained strength, lost succulent leaves
        when flowers faded, shriveled and fell off,
        leaving a skeletal branch, barely alive.

When you were diagnosed with months to live,
        it seemed impossible new growth could come.
When your treatment failed, I threw the plant outside.
Forgotten, it thrived in sandy sunny soil.
New shoots burst through crusty wrinkled appendages
        as your next treatment gave us hope.
Though you became a shadow of yourself,
        a bare skeletal branch, you were
        alive with faith, desperately wanting new growth.

Upon your entry to another world, eternity,
        reclaimed from garden's frost, my cactus thrives.
You have become my Christmas Cactus.

October 22, 1998

My flute teacher gave me a Christmas cactus which bloomed then proceeded to lose its leaves until it was a bare 'Y' shape. I planted it outside before we left for Montana in July. Upon my return, I noticed new growth. Excitement grew within as I hoped Mother's treatment would result in similar growth. Now I know it signifies her heavenly growth. After she died and before the frost, I brought the cactus inside where it continues to thrive.

My son's interpretation of the passage to Heaven.

Passage

Waiting for cancer treatment,
      walking hospital corridors,
      connected to a cell-killing I.V. tower
      trailing behind,
      aided by your loving grandson,
      you walked the mile.
Passage from health to death,
      tunnel to another world,
      long hall windows at either end,
      windows to our world till now,
      corridors of hope lead off to the side,
      you tried to live.
Cancer is rough passage to eternity.

October 22, 1998

"Passage" recalls the two weeks my mother spent at the University of Michigan Hospital for experimental treatment. When we visited her, she was as perky as ever and was dedicated to getting exercise. During walks my pre-adolescent son frequently put his arms around her, carefully pushing her I.V. tower so she would not come unplugged. The tower also carried the chemo drip which continually sent the poison to her liver. I will always remember his tenderness.

35

Jessie Dove reading to her daughter.

The Watch of Jessie Dove (1876-1923)

Do I know the hands that held this watch?
Christmas gift in 1903, dawn of a century.
Rose gold orb, token of love engraved
        amid baroque scrolls for Jessie Dove Pepper.
I've seen her sitting with my grandmother, her daughter,
        in an old brown and white photo, then no more.
That Christmas day when the watch was new
        Jessie smiled a soft rose glow,
        one side opened to "Jessie" DEC 25-03,
        the other revealed a timepiece, intimate display.
Pinned on her lapel by a flower sprouting seed pearls
        and a diamond, Jessie proudly wore the watch.
Nearly a century later I hold her treasure,
        filigreed hands frozen at 1:25, glass cover missing.
What happened to pass the watch on to me?
Who broke the glass, what happened at 1:25?
My own it has become, for just a little while.
In my youth it stayed tucked neatly in grandma's drawer,
        cherished but never worn, forgotten
        until death passed it to my mother's drawer.
Put away for safekeeping, kept for what?
Four generations of women, sharing traits and a watch.
Can this watch tell stories of its owners?
Are we all strong women fighting?
How were we alike? What hills did we climb?
Left only with a frozen watch waiting repair,
        I know we shared more than this golden globe.
I carry parts of each in my soul.

October 22, 1998

"The Watch of Jessie Dove" describes my feelings as the new owner of a family heirloom. I never knew Jessie except through her daughter, my grandmother.

Pressing Swiss Embroidery

I am the "wash and wear" generation.
Wash it. Tumble dry it. Wear it.
Wrinkles were chemically removed.
My clothes always had the crisp look.
Wielding the steam iron was alien,
          gone with the horse and buggy days.
But there you were, pressing night clothes,
          sheets, tablecloths, ruffles, lace.
In your hand the iron glided smoothly
          over stubborn wrinkles on any fabric.
I did not inherit your pride of craft.
Time consuming pressing was not for me.
Sometimes I bought non perma-press,
          tossing freshly cleaned shirts into my pile
          for the day when I had time to iron,
          or to be forgotten, until outgrown.

Now you're gone. I find my iron.
Pressing Swiss embroidery on delicate voile,
          I sense your dedication, determination, power
          to annihilate each crumpled corner.
Satisfaction I gain in smooth sheer fabric
          void of wrinkles, fine cotton deftly woven.
A tedious job becomes a memory of you.
I want to iron my pain away.
Remembrance smoothes my grief.
Pressing fine fabric brings me closer to you.
Together we iron in parallel worlds,
          intersecting in everyday memories.
Your craft becomes my joy.

October 26, 1998

I hate pressing, but found new joy and maternal connections. I could not get enough of it that day.

39

Last Table at Knight's

Who would know this would be her last
    meal out at the local steakhouse?
We walked through a dark smoky area,
       past the table celebrating school's end,
       the table of my birthday, months before
       when I wore her dress evoking strangers' compliments.
We walked amid bustle and hubbub, everyone busy
       eating, living their lives, ours becoming a blur.
To the paneled non-smoker's room we walked
       to the last corner table beneath pictures of coaches
       smiling at their triumphant victories.

This meal became her small triumph,
       just being there at the last table
       in her roomy cotton dress I made
       revealing her skinny arms, cancer casualties.
I noticed she didn't fit here either.
I sensed, did not understand until she was gone.
At the last table at Knight's joining friends
       in slow motion style her smile was stretched.
Not the energetic, vibrant person she was
       caught in disease warp dimension
       while normal people dined and talked.
Between worlds we were desperately trying
       to reclaim life's normalcy.
Out of place as the wig on her head,
       she sat straight in her chair, calculating
       each bite while others ate and talked.
There, but not there, at that table at Knight's.

Her delicate smile, less than half-eaten burger,
        untouched salad, onion rings, now are memories.
'Twas her last venture into the land of the living,
        bittersweet that dinner at Knight's.
She was dying then and we didn't know it.
Wanting to live, she bought that last meal.
She tried to stay but just couldn't last
        at Knight's table where the burgers are big.
In cancer's corner she fought, most unfair disadvantage.
I saw it at Knight's backroom table, her fight to sit high.
That corner became a culmination of her will
        to go out, continue living as long as she could.

She's gone from the table now, gone from this world.
At night I feel her smiling down on me, finally victorious.
Strengthened, I continue living past my heart's grief.
Someday I'll return to that last table at Knight's.

                              October 27, 1998

    *This was a spur-of-the-moment dinner outing at Knight's Steak
House in Ann Arbor. After reeling from chemotherapy, Mother fi-
nally felt well enough to go out to eat. We bumped into good friends
who joined us at our table. It became her last meal out. She loved
dining out, which was a major part of my childhood.*

Spider on My Windshield

Spider on my windshield, hanging, I drive away.
Window-secured by invisible thread,
     breeze flapping spider, going faster,
     becoming a sleek gray aerodynamic bullet
     connected to my car, piercing the wind.
I stop. Spider resumes normal greenish shape,
     commences glass walking, looking for home.
Have I taken it from family and friends?
Main road, I accelerate. Spider assumes bullet pose.
How versatile, adapting to moving wind
     while I ride inside climate-controlled comfort.
How long can he cling to my moving vehicle?
How many more stowaways have I displaced?

And then, I think of you, bracing for the ride
     through cancer, chemo, radiation, and back.
You adapted, spider-like, changing shape and color
     hanging on to life dear, losing weight, turning pale.
Normal bodies fueled our stressful trip, helpless
     while you were separated by cancer's window.
What hope held you on those frequent frightful rides?

I turn my attention to the fall color-graced road,

gaining top speed, unaware my spider slipped away

unable to hold any longer to my racing car.

You, too, slipped away amid autumn's brilliant display

unable to hold on any more to your racing world.

You fought the fight, held tight, adapted, adjusted.

You became versatile like my spider hitch-hiker.

Free in the firmament, displaced no more,

you are secure in heaven's greatest rooms

welcoming tomorrow's displaced stowaways.

October 29, 1998

A creamy transparent green spider hitch-hiked a ride on my car one autumn day.

The Inn Keeper's Wife

It's the busiest of nights at our Inn there's no room.
Traveling to Bethlehem weary souls from afar,
     we feed them and board them, they stay at our Inn
     while I cook up fresh porridge, stew, and roast meat.
They come rich and poor to stay at our Inn,
     extra mats on the floor for all to lie down.
On this busy cool night there's a star shining bright.
White streaks from heaven hover high overhead.
We turn people away, no room at the Inn.
Where else could they stay except the barn with the hay?
One couple comes late, weary, she bulging with babe.
No room in her belly. What could we do?
Food we have plenty, mats we have none.
We must turn them away. Must we refuse?
Remembering the star and the barn way out back,
     I plead with my man to let them stay there.
"No room at the Inn," I hear him say in the night,
     "but you may stay there with the cows in the barn."
Both of us sense the brightness shining straight above
     is more than ordinary starlight in the night.
Angels sing, shepherds come. Inside others stay warm.
I leave my guests, taking gifts of food to the barn.
My heart's outside with new birth. What can this mean?
Sudden joy fills my soul. Can this be the birth of a king?
The world is so busy. What part do we play?
We've no rooms left inside but the rooms of our hearts.

November 2, 1998

*One year earlier my mother participated in the church advent
dinner theater. We were guests at the Inn. She was the inn keeper's
wife and convinced her husband to let the holy couple use the stable
for the night. A delightful event.*

Dinner theater, Westminster Presbyterian Church, 1997.

Last Words

It will be too late.

You better come now.

Come by my side.

I don't think I can wait.

It will be okay with just the three of us.

I don't know how to do this, take my last breath.

I'm thirsty.

> Do you want a drink?

> What would you like?

My family.

Hi! I'm still here!

You take a nap.

If I take a nap, it doesn't mean I...

I don't think I can wait.

> Wait for what?

For her to come.

Please just let me go.

I don't want to stay.

How much longer will this [dying] take?

> Just relax and let go.

Check if it's okay.

> If what's okay?

You know...

It's okay for you to go.

Aw, you know I can't go anywhere.

Is it okay [for a child to be here]?

It's okay, he knows.

I'm not ready to go yet.

Your purple and green look pretty together.

I'll be here in twenty years for your wedding.

Betsy-Susie!

(frail arms hug granddaughter)

Please wait...

Let me go.

I want to go home.

We'll love you for eternity.

November 3, 1998

At her death, Mother was still so full of life and very alert. Always a mother, she was concerned to have my son witness her death and wanted to be sure it was okay for him to be present. "Last Words" is really her poem. I just recorded and arranged her final words. She died less than an hour later.

47

Sympathy Cards

When sympathy cards stop coming
      is it time to stop crying?
Does grief end on a certain date
      when we get busy with life?
Too much time passes.
It does not lessen my pain.
I read each card with notes inside.
Opening pages turns a release valve.
Memories pour from the card and my heart
      melting into shimmering soul-cleansing tears.
I cry with each card, remembering a life lived.
Is that life forgotten when cards stop appearing?
What more can be said than what's already written
      by countless people connected through death?
Cards come in all sizes, colors, and verses.
Handwritten memories stir my heart best.
Some contain surprises, acts of kindness I'd never known,
      cards from strangers telling me how they
      were touched.
Must I stop crying when the tide subsides?
Tears wrench me, cleanse me, free me from pain.

My grief extends beyond months of mourning.

When the cards stop coming I'll just open them again.

I'll cry and remember, feel, and sit still

    letting tears flow freely into a river.

Joy for a life lived becomes part of me.

Some day I'll put the cards all away,

    safely keeping her in my heart.

November 3, 1998

I could not open sympathy cards quickly enough in order to read their contents, especially remembrances. Whereas my sister hoarded hers until she could read them and cry, I cried with each one still looking for more in my mailbox the next day. Now I know to send cards to others at any time.

New Plantings

Nothing is solid, everything changes.
Falling leaves bid adieu to summer.
Sad good-byes grace your exit.
New plantings replace diseased growth.
Hope springs anew from fresh shoots.
We plant new trees in your memory
    suggesting your many colors.
Weeping Cherry for our sadness,
    your anxiety from worry.
Pink your passion for living,
    your cascading inner beauty.
Sugar Maple bursting with color
    just as you did
    in your vivacity
    and fun-loving ways.
Everything changes, nothing remains.
New plantings will remind us of you.
They'll change with the seasons
    hinting at your changes, physical to spirit.
Fallen leaves bid adieu to this world.
Preparing spring's rebirth, remembrance,
    we plant your spirit in our hearts.

November 4, 1998

I wanted to plant a Weeping Cherry tree in memory of my mother. My dad planted one for her a few years ago. My son wanted the Sugar Maple. He liked the vibrant colors which reminded him of his grandmother. We ended up planting a Star Magnolia.

Souvenirs

Champion of world bazaars, she collected
    souvenirs, travel remembrances,
    T-shirts from everywhere:
    Paris, Rhodes, Australia, Boston,
    Boca Grande, Montana, New York,
    Switzerland, Alaska, Hawaii.
She bought trinkets and priceless
    fine white sand, shells, and sea dollars,
    Norwegian sweaters, Mexican flutes,
    silver charms for her bracelets, Scottish dolls,
    British "Bobby" hats, stuffed bears,
    fine French perfume, German woodcarvings.
Armed with tour books, guide books, language books,
    menus, beer coasters, foreign currency,
    hotel complimentary soaps, toiletries
    in her purse of Mary Poppins proportions,
    she brought the world home to us.
Novel tourist, ageless and fearless,
    modern conqueror of Grand Canyon mules,
    Caribbean cruises: Aruba, Nassau, Bahamas,
    courageous Windjammer, burning plane jumper.
What remembrances of her do we now hold?

Well-worn shirts of worldwide manufacture,

      a hand-spun New Zealand woolen vest,

      Aborigine Dirigidoo, Williamsburg fife replica.

She sent us the world via postcards

      marked with arrows pinpointing her room

      always telling us we'd love it there.

We'd have to come sometime and never did.

We met her once at Tivoli after her mother died

      and I was abroad missing the wake.

I wasn't ready for death then, half a world away.

I've seen the world through her souvenirs since then.

Now her collections remind me of her.

November 6, 1998

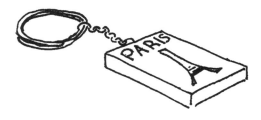

We gradually convinced Mother to stop bringing us souvenirs from her travels. She continued, bringing only T-shirts and keychains which are even more special now. My father really liked this poem.

Riding Past Grief

Quietness surrounds her contemplative persona.

Six weeks past from the Pinery she rushed

    to ailing grandmother's bedside,

    unaware her last hug it would be.

The dying one waited for her return,

    leaving this world shortly thereafter.

Tears were shed, mementos were found,

    especially those things with *the grandma smell.*

Wearing grandma's dress at memorial service,

    she grew up sparkling her grandmother's joy.

Cousins and aunts shared in the mourning.

Food sent by others helped us focus on being.

Back to school and living life,

    it's not every day you lose a grandmother.

And so the days went missing a presence,

    nose back in books, mind quietly busy,

    shedding dry tears, silently grieving.

She crafted an angel of copper bright wire.

Hung in her room, Joanne's angel was home.

Not much was said of her loss or her sorrow.

Youth does not know how to mourn death.

Homebound, carpool with kids after school,

safe haven for riding past grief.

Turning a corner to the school where grandma taught,

"There's grandma's room" she said quite aloud,

a connection in seconds midst riding on memories.

No one else noticed, once it was out

as natural as anything, innocent memory.

She's grieving as kids do, in their own way.

Small connections become milestones.

November 7, 1998

I was concerned how my daughter was dealing with her grandmother's death. She never wanted to talk about it, but admitted she was grumpy because of it. The events in this poem occurred while my daughter was coming home from school. I would have missed it, but my friend, who was driving, shared this precious moment.

Joanne's classroom at Forsythe Middle School, Ann Arbor, Michigan. Years later, her granddaughter would see this room from the viewpoint of the car in the window.

November Winds

November winds strip trees bare.
Gale forces disturb my shelter.
Pitch blackness surges bright green light,
    entire sky arching in electronic charges.
Current alive, land pulsing,
    my house hums in whipping wind.
Inside, we ignore building stress noises,
    creaking, groaning, massive invisible onslaught.
Next morn awake I to a littered lawn,
    nature's pruned debris to be collected.
I gather my thoughts in death's aftermath.
November winds dare disturb my shelter.
Your memories are heart-vault secure.
Storm clouds part, blue skies beyond.
No threatening gray clouds where you are.
My face feels sun-cast light warm.
Once blocked from view, now I see
    blazing sun through silhouetted trees.
Stripped of all, unburdened, they reach up.
Sturdy trunks store summer's harvest
    for the long winter to come.
Still sun flames across empty boughs
    gracing new light upon craggy growth,
    living stored for better times.
November winds prune back my life.

November 12, 1998

"November Winds" was inspired by an inland hurricane we had two days before my last dissertation recital.

Between Waking and Sleeping

I tried taking a nap, ended up having a vision.

It was more than "Hello" when she appeared to me

in that state of sleep where you think you

are not asleep

but you really are, where you want to

move your arms

and think you are, but you really aren't.

That kind of state.

That's where I met her, between waking and sleeping.

She held my left hand and I hers, limp but warm,

as it felt in my hand right after death.

In my left ear she spoke while holding my hand.

So real, as if living again speaking to me.

I wish I knew exactly what she was saying, but cannot recall.

I regret the times when alive she did talk; I did not listen.

I was listening today, just couldn't remember after she left.

It had something to do with my arm hurting, but more than that.

She encouraged me to continue even though I have pain.

It is more than my forearm, but a pain in my heart.

How do I know she spoke to me?

Awake by now, I shed a tear, looked at my clock.

It was 4:20, her departing time.

Then I knew I was in another zone,

a meeting place between dreams and earthly living.

She's gone now.

But, I know I will see her again,

      sometime between waking and sleeping.

She will come to me, speaking my heart.

I have someplace to return when living is tough.

It will stop hurting in that in-between place.

November 15, 1998

*My right arm hurt while practicing for my dissertation recital.
As I rested, this vision became one of many in which I felt Mother's
healing love.*

Last Trip

Steamboating down the mighty Mississippi
    following Mark Twain's path.
Watch a show onboard, stay up late,
    retire to stately room with balcony.
Paddle wheel goes round and round.
Calliope tune pipes on your way
    to New Orleans, Mardi Gras revelry.
Just seven months for you to live.
Unknown cancer grew within.
What more was there to do?
You did it all ebulliently.
Your boat steamed full ahead.
Life's rivers gave passage,
    just missed by violent tornado.
Was it an omen to pass you by,
    giving you time to collect baggage,
    keeping only cherished essentials?
That last trip is but a refrigerator postcard.
The Mississippi Queen carries your joy
    around and around up river and down.
A monument to your travels in a postcard.
Last one I'll get from you.

November 15, 1998

A postcard of my parents' last trip caught my attention. It hung on my refrigerator door all summer, the last thing Mother sent me.

Joanne and Claude in front of the Mississippi Queen,
February 27, 1998.

A Chocolate Moment

It was a chocolate moment
        aroused by sweet aroma.
Palatal senses prepare,
        plunge into richness,
        thick, full, savory.
You lived as a moment
        savoring its sweetness
        even when it melted,
        cancer-ravaged gooey mess.
Chocolate, still appreciated,
        became gifts to others.
When I bite into candy
        the sugar stirs, zings me
        into a momentary high.
Meeting you in chocolate moments,
        your joy coats my sorrow.
Everyone knew your weakness.
You lived a chocolate moment.

November 18, 1998

Mother was a chocoholic. It was the one thing she would eat during chemotherapy treatment. Lots of people showered her with chocolates. After daintily nibbling on one, she ended up giving the rest to my children.

Dirty Laundry

My life is a mountain of laundry piled high.
Countless baskets of the stuff threaten my existence.
Unlike miller's daughter locked in King's dungeon,
  no Rumpelstiltskin spins my hay into gold.
I'm on my own, cleaning other people's dirt.
Why am I locked in this impossible task?
I've my own dirty laundry to do.
How many times did I hang up on her
  while she was talking but would not listen?
Or the times I wished she were out of my life?
She's gone now. I sit amid piles of soiled linen.
Sorted. Folded. Stored. Clean clothes don't need laundering.
I've scaled the mountain, basket by basket, again and again,
  as I did with a mother's seemingly meddling pestering ways.
We sorted, washed out our hidden laundry piles.
Dark stains removed by bleached determination.
Mending tears in our bond, our fabric became brighter.
Air-dried in soft soothing sunny breezes,
  I benefit now from dust- and moth-free closets.
Mended, restored, our lives became fine crisp linen.
Until cancer dared eat it all away.
Washed, dirty laundry waits for days beyond need.
So, I continue washing, sorting, putting away filth.
Grief cleanses my heart's dungeon dark room.
Clean clothing gives a welcome freshness.
Mountains of laundry eventually disappear,
  revealing her stored treasure in my heart.

        November 22, 1998

*After my third dissertation recital and oral examinations, I had
a mountain of laundry in my closet. It took a week to conquer.*

The Perfect Christmas

Every year well before snowfall
    the Christmas bug would invade.
Long before commercials appeared on T.V.,
    a list would be made of purchases bought,
    for whom, how much, what, and where hid.
Consumer's way of keeping Christmas year-round.
Soon after Thanksgiving the house would be decked,
    sparkling white lights twinkling on bushes outside.
Everyone knew this house was special.

Hand-dipped candles were painted for advent.
Out came the crèche, true holiday symbol.
Then came the carolers crafted with care,
    old Rudolph, Santa's irresistible sleigh, electric angel.
Trinkets of last year's clearance came next,
    happy mixture of past holiday celebrations
    on display for a season.
Neat lists of gifts, food, festivities, kept things in order.
Lists to ensure no thing was forgotten,
    right down to the meal, table, and china.
Stuffing ingredients always the same,
    cornbread, olives, and oysters, secret ingredient,
    reminder of seventeen years East.
We had to do this and had to do that.
Go visit Santa in his cardboard display.
Must read Clements' poem, leave cookies and milk.
When did we celebrate the real reason for mirth?

It was the same year after year, always
    the perfect Christmas observed.

Gracious hostess, Mrs. Christmas, my mother.
Much money and time went in the planning.
What would Jesus think if he came back to all this?
Would he topple the trees, lights, and bows in his palace
        as he did in the temple at angry tax men?
Down would come angels of crystal and silver,
        stars of all kinds, stables, and mangers.
Lists would be burnt, money sent to the poor,
        reminding us Christmas comes to each heart
        near or far.
Decorated or not we must open our doors,
        not cram them with cherries.
Just exactly what IS the perfect Christmas?

She's finding out herself up in heaven.
Who would have thought she'd be there so soon?
What Christmas celebration does heaven observe?
We know there are angels singing God's glory.
Are trees dressed in their own decorations?
Does heaven need Christmas commercialization?
How I wish she could send us a message
        telling us how they celebrate up there.
Gone the commercials, the bells ringing money,
        busy shoppers shopping, forgetting the reason.
Stripped of all excess, heaven does it just right.
The perfect Christmas will be spent in His sight.
She's finally doing Christmas perfect at last.

                                November 30, 1998

Joanne, Christmas 1935

. . . . and 1992.

Mother usually started her Christmas "to do" list in early fall.
After her death, we never found the list that went with the presents
she bought in advance. We had other things on our minds.

New Moon Rising

New moon rising on pillow soft clouds.
My hopes rise above driving pain
    darkened by watermarked grey sky.
We see the same moon from different worlds.
Is the man in the moon heaven's gatekeeper
    or the Gibson girl mourning my loss?
Still the moon rises, shedding its glow
    whispering white light on the earth below.
I feel your love in the rising moontide.

New moon rising on grief-filled living,
    shedding soft light on new dimensions of being.
Moonglow creates an in-between world.
Life stretches beyond mortal frontiers.
I sense your peace, fulfillment, and healing.
My hopes rise on silky soft moonbeams,
    your harmony sent straight to my heart.

December 4, 1998

New moon, full moon, is a full moon viewed from earth a new moon in heaven? Mother's death opened new world possibilities for me. There is more to life than I can comprehend. We just live in different worlds that do not connect, or do they?

Angel Joanne

Guardian angels assigned at birth
    take on our names, I imagine.
We meet at death, joining in teamwork
    sending encouraging messages earthside--
    love, protection--from eternity to now.
Here in misery we fashioned an angel
    reminiscent of our mother, grandmother, friend.
Angel Joanne made of bright copper wire,
    happy shiny fiery ebullient sparkles and more.
Twisted, shaped in this life she was formed.
Cork screw curls, big transparent lifting wings,
    outstretched arms gather us in.
Feet dangle free. She floats in the air.

Angel Joanne reminds us of hope,
      loving and living, her enthusiasm, vibrancy,
      calling us to continue living and working.
Someday we'll meet our own angels.
Then Angel Joanne will flutter a welcome
      briefing us on work to be done.
Life never stops, but continues
      in heavenly proportions.
We just can't see beyond
      death's iron-clad curtain.
Guardian angels always keep in touch.
Hush, if you're quiet you can hear for yourself.
There's Angel Joanne whistling new tunes.
Glory for God and a life well lived.

December 4, 1998

My daughter made a copper wire angel during grief work at Arbor Hospice. She has not talked much about her grandmother's death, but the angel hangs by her bed.

Last Rose

The last rose she beheld
      grew in my garden
      blooming for her departure.
Yellow glow petals
      tenderly caressed buttercup days
      drooping farewell sadness.
She smelled its fullness,
      wilting upon her death.
Not a petal lost,
      each dried shriveled
      around the core
      suffocating summer's abundance.
Mourning her passing,
      emptied of tears,
      I have that last rose
      upon my windowsill,
      reminder of fleeting glory.

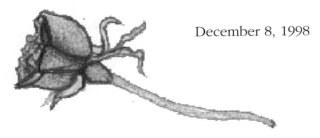

December 8, 1998

The evening my mother entered Hospice I brought roses from my garden. She briefly noted their beauty as I presented them. One dried naturally. I kept it on my windowsill all winter as a reminder.

Everything Right

Hard being a perfectionist.
Nothing is straight.
Asymmetry rules.
Anxiety builds our shortcomings.
Perfect in an imperfect world is tough.
Too many variables.
We never measure up,
       even to our own standards.

December 8, 1998

We always had difficulty living up to Mother's perfectionist expectations. She even did. In the end, it really did not matter if things were done correctly. There is no right way when it comes to dying.

Holding Angel Hands

Again, we met in dream,
    alive before cancer's claim,
    watching signs of its spread.
You would know it had your brain
    when no longer you speak right,
    so warned the doctor.
You looked at me from the past.
The future knew the truth.
Transversing time, I reached
    from now to yesterday.
Time froze.
Across dimensions I took your hand,
    told of your death, alert and talkative.
Doctor erred, your speech stayed right
    to the end. You understood.
In vision meeting your warm hand
    radiated power, light from you to me,
    transfusion of your heavenly energy.
Knowing you reached from beyond,
    I was holding angel hands.

December 16, 1998

An extremely comforting dream on my sister's birthday. In real life Mother's doctors did not say anything about her brain or speech. They had nothing but compassion and admiration for her.

Grief Tears

Grief tears are toxic.
They're hot and they sting,
    make your face red,
    make your heart burn.
They come without warning.
Toxic tears compress outsides within
    tightly pressed blocks steaming you flat.
Tears drain, running warm on dry skin
    ceaselessly dripping down cavernous cheeks.
My tears contort, stretch me, and pinch.
Rivers blocked by stiff dams,
    I try to keep going, keep happy, to smile.
Grief tears harass joy, peace, and living.
Flow free my tears, oceans of sorrow.
What can be left when they fill past the brim?
Toxic tears dilute in fresh living water.
Tears turn crystal clear cool in the light.
My tears scream out my loss.
Toxic grief tears must run their course.
Tears carry pollution away from my soul.

December 20, 1998

My father and I attended a seminar at Arbor Hospice. We were pleasantly surprised to discover we were on the right road to processing Mother's death and our grief. It still hurts, but I know it is cleansing.

Cancer Journey

Journey to the other side,
    cancer journey,
    losing a mother,
    passage to a place
    where I cannot go,
    impervious boundary.

I needed rest, a break.
Instead, my heart breaks.
Cancer, death,
    ugly reality, unreal dream,
    there is no escape,
    no medical cure.
Emotional cancer spreads
    as toxic worry.
Shell-shocked from diagnosis,
    looking for another world,
    obsessed with living
    like nothing else matters,
    cancer affects us all.

December 22, 1998

The director of Arbor Hospice invited me to write a chapter for her book on dying. These were my initial thoughts as I started to write.

Grandma's Ring

I didn't understand why she wore that ring
    clutched in her hand the day her mother died,
    ordinary engagement ring set in platinum.
My mother wore grandma's ring as her own.

Now I wear the ring in familiar setting,
    eighty-year gem, old-fashioned cut,
    worn by three generations of women.
With it I feel balanced, complete.

I understand why she wore the ring,
    feeling her presence since first slipping it on,
    memories of women forging before me,
    diamond on each hand, today
    next to yesterday.

January 1, 1999

I never expected to find comfort in a ring. I remember it well upon both women before me.

Life Poems

The world is a poem waiting to be written.
Fragments flutter through my head
      caught only by a pencil-net.
I wrote my life on scraps of paper,
      the girl who couldn't stop writing.
Perhaps someday they will be preserved,
      lifework shelved in library stacks.
Will others know their meanings to me,
      how they preserved my life?
Life poems become sanctuary.

January 4, 1999

Poems quickly became part of my own grief therapy. I shared them with my father, family, and friends. I also found they helped others deal with their own losses.

Two Necklaces

From her jewel box I chose
    a necklace, shortly after she died.
Amid precious finery I found it,
    simple multi-strands of gold-tones
    carrying tiny reflective squares.
It spoke to me in unsung language.
Round my neck it hung for her funeral,
    simple, feminine, wistful reminder,
    my favorite of her collection.

Holidays passed, her presence missed.
I received her belated gift
    wrapped by widower hands.
Surprised, I beheld the same necklace,
    simple, reflective of our bond.
Two necklaces I now have.
We chose alike unknowingly.
One worn in memorial,
    another in anniversary,
    sparkling soul testimony.

January 4, 1999

My father gave me a necklace Mother purchased for our anniversary. I was ever aware of the mother-daughter bond as I opened the gift. Evidently, she purchased the same necklace for herself which I picked out of her jewelry box to wear for her memorial service. Out of all her jewelry, I chose the same one she had chosen for me.

Winter Rainbow

I followed the rainbow home one frigid winter day.
It led the way, peering through a cloudy sucker hole,
     surreal 3-D colors shining on dismal gray clouds.
Did everyone see the bright sky-prism,
     or was it a message for my eyes only?
Just a portion of vibrant colors shone that day,
     stripes of light emblazoned in the sky,
     effervescent for awhile, and then gone.
Was I imagining the peculiar occurrence?
Where was the rain in below-zero temperatures?
I beheld the blazing sun close to the horizon
     realizing God's skyborn promise would soon disappear,
     a connection, perhaps, between two worlds
     appearing at her dying time, when the sun dies too.
Winter rainbow on my horizon becomes a promise,
     a porthole to better worlds where hearts are not heavy.
Complete rainbows will fill my life, abolishing sorrow.
In a place where winter rainbows circle the earth,
     I will see them all in this world beyond worlds.
Long after sunset, my winter rainbow lives within.

                          January 5, 1999

I was on my way home from driving my daughter across town after school. Driving to the west, I saw a most spectacular portion of a rainbow peeking through a small clearing in the clouds. It was one of those sub-zero days when I felt a warm connection to my mother.

The Bumblebee

Warm sunny lazy summer day...
    buzzing bees leave gold fluffs on my driveway.
Big yellow fuzzy black bumblebee
    crawling on the black-top.
Child-like, I smash him,
    smooshing bee guts into hot asphalt.
Horrified by my actions, I wonder...
Are you like the bee
    minding your own business?
Will you be snuffed by a big foot
    from another dimension?
Choosing ignorance, I go my way.

Another sunny hot lazy day...
    another fat buzzing bee
    on its back furiously circling
    trying to set free of its condition.
Remembering my folly, I reach...
    setting it free by broom handle.
Off he flew without looking back.
No "thanks," up to safety he went.

This happened to you...
    buzzing futilely, trying to live,
    to be freed from cancer.
You left all too soon.
Unlike the bee, you looked back
    where you'd been knowing
    safety and home in the heavens.

January 15, 1999

This happened in August when I was leaving to visit my mother in the hospital. At the time, I felt encouraged, but later realized my mother already had had her second chance fifteen years earlier surviving breast cancer.

American Laundromat

Sitting in a laundromat, in America,
    washing my sorrows away,
    I stare and stare at rows of portholes,
    silver diver's gear of yesteryear.
I load my soiled rugs in
    triple loader washer extractors,
    slam the door on yesterday's filth.
Armed with plenty of quarters and soap,
    Texas-sized machines flood violently
    beyond locked glass doors.
I wait for the cycle to end
    listening to radio America.
I am outside looking in.
Water sloshes up around and down.
Cycle done, I feed hungry giant dryer
    emptying more coins from my pocket.
Computerized dryer tosses my rugs
    baked at high temperatures.
I am mesmerized by repetitive action.
My rugs are lighter, cleaner as they dry,
    emerging fresh for tomorrow's foot traffic.
When will I emerge lighter, fresher
    from grief's pillage and pain?

January 31, 1999

We had our share of plumbing disasters during a month of deep snow. I took our rugs to the laundromat and had time to think.

We Live Where

We live where our belongings are,
    heaps of personal effects on life's journey.
Our homes become storage facilities
    for yesterday's collections.
Temporary shelters from birth to death,
    we live where our hearts take us.

February 1, 1999

I know Mother has just changed residences. In dealing with all her earthly possessions left behind, I realize it is not our things that make a house our home, but our hearts.

Joanne's homes

If I to Die Tomorrow

If I to die tomorrow,
    I want the world to know
    more to life than sex and sin.
We die on earth but just begin
    to live with angels, eternal bliss
    while scorners reject and hiss.
I found a mole upon my breast.
It worried me unto unrest.
What pain lurks below dark spots
    goes deeper tying stomach knots.
My voice gets louder as I cry
    about lost time until I die.
Wasted days on nothing and everything,
    forever, I want to dance and sing.
And so I shall if I to die
    for I will be on high.
Ushered to another world,
    peace in me will be unfurled.

February 2, 1999

My try at rhyme as I try to make sense of life and death. Death stirs up questions about life as those left behind try to understand the unknown.

How's Life?

Here was a lady leading full life,
        worked for a living teaching teens words.
Words held power on paper and sound
        keeping her connected by phone and by book.
How's life? was a question asked many a time.
Life's busy with children, teaching, and playing,
        eating with friends, shopping with Mother.
Life was easy, just live it and thrive
        following rules passed from parent to child.

Then came a day when retired she paused
        too busy, family photos by drawers remain unnamed.
How's life? At this point it was busy
        going from points far and farther still,
        still managing time for her family, her joy.
Time was spent shopping, traveling, watching, dining.
What's more important in life than to do this?
Life was easy to live, abundantly full.
Too full, perhaps, leaving no time for self.

Another day came when her life came to a halt,
        shortened by cancer in spite of her wishes.
Sometimes I imagine her life up above
        what it is like, how she is living.
How's life in heaven? The question rebounds.
I can just hear her giggle, too busy to answer,
        busy living up to her true potential.
All I can say is God knew all this.
This super-charged woman now lives in His care.

How's life? I ask of the wintery clouds,
 knowing she's there airing them out
  spreading her joy around other dimensions.
How's life? I ask of myself in need of bright joy.
Send some to me to lighten my load.
My life, busy too, keeps a door open
 for God's peace to keep lighting my way.

February 16, 1999

"How's Life?" catches one of my many moments wondering how my mother is enjoying Heaven.

Last Kiss

We came in to see her on her death-bed
        hours after she crossed to her new world.
There she lay in a warm candle-lit room.
We gathered 'round in mournful respect.
A song was sung into unhearing ears.
Released from cancer's pain she was free,
        free of the worry, free of this world,
        gone to a place oft times I wanted to go.
She lay still tucked in pale pink sheets.
A fresh rose lay on her unmoving breast.
I never imagined this day would appear,
        last day for living, for saying good-bye.

How do you bid adieu to a mother
        who bore you, raised you, loved you, and more?
Words are inadequate, touch loses meaning.
How do we let go with no release valve?
It happens regardless as time marches on.
We'd best join the beat and step right in line.
But marching to where when life ends for one?
I'd rather just crash, thrash, and cry.

We gathered one last time, my family and I.
My father said "good-bye" as always he did,
        then bent down and kissed the corpse
        of his wife.
I noticed a reticence, no lingering smooch.
The kiss left him cold as her body that night.

Gone was the warmth, response, vitality.
Last kiss robbed him of warm loving memories
        becoming a cold nothing, devastating surprise.

Now it's a memory, last kiss, good or bad.
Past kisses will have to be remembered,
        replacing weak ways of saying farewell.
We really don't know how to say good-bye
        or know when last kisses will be forever.

February 16, 1999

Many months after her death, my father told me how surprised he was by that last kiss. He called it a disaster.

Joanne and her girls on Peconic Bay,
Long Island, New York, circa 1958.

The Su-De was a row boat my sister and I used every summer on Peconic Bay, at the end of Long Island, New York. My early childhood memories of these summers are rich as if they happened yesterday. The boat still hangs in my parents' garage in Michigan.

Su-De

Oh the Su-De was a sturdy little dinghy:
    white rowboat, two oars and three seats
    with a canvas bumper all the way around.
We set off to sea in the boat Su-De
    on a summer's day on Peconic Bay.
Water below, blue skies above,
    we cast our rods where little fish bite,
    bobbing bouys from our wooden row boat,
    salt water below, dry taste on our lips,
    searching the depths on a lazy hot day.
Fish tug our lines. We fling them on board.
Blowfish bounty-laden, we head for shore.
Releasing most, our catch swims fast away.
A few saved for game, playing toss in the air,
    prickly wet skin lands in my palms
    while frightened fish fly in the air.
Soon set free, they flee for deeper haven.
Named for a mother's two daughters,
    the stout Su-De carried many a load.
The boat brought us carefree days.
Dry-docked inland, still painted fresh white,
    memories now bouy us over turbulent waters.
Gone are lazy sunny days of unconcern.
Briny taste remains, powdery fine.
Puffed up like our safety-seeking blowfish,
    we camouflage our weaknesses,
    seeking deep waters of hope.
Now two daughters remain on shore
    knowing their mother found safety afar,
    while the dinghy keeps memories afloat.

                          Februrary 16, 1999

Looking for Living

Each time I go there I'm looking for something,
       a reminder, a message, I don't quite know what.
I open her closets, pull out her drawers,
       look through the contents, searching for nothing.
Dresser drawers they are full, but me I am empty.
I don't know what I'm seeking, why I am searching.
Driving her car, wearing her coat, I seek clues,
       messages left behind from mother to daughter.
We use things on earth taking nothing beyond.
Maybe I'm seeking a message from there.
Our possessions are just borrowed for awhile.
All her belongings are mine if I want them,
       though none replace her smile or vivacity.
Maybe I'm hoping for some sign of life.
Nothing remains but unworn clothing,
       old books, and knick-knacks.
Looking for living, a purpose, a reason,
       my unknown quest lures me somewhere within.
It is there where she lives in my heart.
We are more than our things gathered in life.

February 22, 1999

It seems every time I went over to my parents' house after Mother's death I was looking for something and could not find it. Problem was, I did not know what I was looking for. Now I realize I will always be looking for signs of my mother, still alive.

Lifetime of Holidays

We lived a lifetime of holidays in one short summer.
From diagnosis through illness to death, we lived them all.
It began during spring's rebirth, her sudden cancer
    robbed us of the joys of a mended relationship.
When we could have been lunching, we were crying
    for more time, to watch kids grow,
    celebrate holidays together.
We searched the past for tomorrow's hope.
Watching old family movies with no sound,
    the old times played before us in a darkened room.
Gone were yesterday's youthful sounds.
Birthday celebrations, Christmas, and Easter observed
    same way year after year, marked only
    by our growth.
Macy's 50's fashion parade in our 90's home.
Decorated trees and eggs, lots of toys and stuffed animals,
    where was the real meaning behind the merriment?
Thus, we celebrated a lifetime of holidays
    observed in the same way year after year.
Until she died. Then we changed the game.
Did we waste our time on holidays ill observed?
Now we celebrate truth and victory over death.
A lifetime of holidays continues into new tomorrows.

                                    March 3, 1999

We had fun watching old home movies during Mother's illness. Labor Day was her last holiday when she could barely walk between two driveways on our street. That was the last time she came over. She died two weeks before her October birthday. Thanksgiving followed the next month, Christmas thereafter, and their January anniversary. Thus, were we thrust right into the holidays after her death.

Wednesday Night Live

Together in fellowship at church one winter's eve,
 families gather, dine, and share mid-week,
 sheltering homeless in warm community,
 continuing Christ's mission, caring for others.
In darkness I stand outside the merry window.
Separated by glass, I cannot hear inside
 or feel warmth from the snow-covered garden.
Outside the goldfish bowl I watch others move
 like watching an old home movie with no sound.
Full color, life before me, I cannot touch or hear.
I can only see from afar, separated by glass barrier.
Memorial garden guards the entrance to the living church.
Feeling presence of sleeping souls in the still snow,
 it is from this place I view life--pure, sparkling, silent.
Those who walked before cannot cross heavenly boundaries.
Opening the door, I enter, releasing brief sound waves outside.
Inside the room liquid warmth surrounds my senses.
Inside my soul I remain connected to those outside.
We are more than those present at the meal.

March 3, 1999

Our church's mid-week family program is called "Wednesday Night Live", a time of meal, choir rehearsals, lessons, and fellowship. My parents and family have attended these evenings for years. I parked the car and before entering the church walked past the memorial garden where Mother's remains are interred. It was then that I felt the buried saints' presence.

Blood and Paper

Red and white, liquid and stiff,
     lifeblood flows as water.
Paper yellows and crumbles.
Water nourishes, feeds, cleanses.
Manufactured paper dissolves in water.
Lifeblood flows, lifeblood grows.
New life begins in floating womb.
Wedded rights confirmed on paper,
     man-made contracts a commitment.
A daughter is blood connected by birth,
     a husband by paper, void at death.
Umbilical bonds remain forever.
Death frees a spouse for other mates
     turning a daughter's life inside out.
A husband loses a soul mate,
     a daughter, her mother-friend.
Blood still flows while paper burns.
Does death really release marriage bonds?
Fifty years together do not evaporate.
Lifeblood flows, memories flood old papers.
Vows remain an unbroken soul bond.
A daughter finds hidden maternal connections
     while a spouse strives to fill a massive void.
Her blood persists in me, his marriage in memories.
Death destroys neither blood nor paper.
Blood continues living through progeny.
Paper is forgotten in yesterday's scrapbook.

March 11, 1999

This ugly little poem vented my anger when my father began seeing other women. In middle age I became intensely aware of how children of divorce must feel when a parent begins dating. While I do not want to deny my father happiness, I must contend with my own feelings. Ironically, upon reading this poem, my father quickly snatched it up to proudly include in his collection.

When a Mother Dies

An unwelcome journey begins in maternal void.
Motherless daughters embark upon uncharted trails.
Orphaned, disconnected with the past and all hope,
> grief surges swell, flooding me with
> heart searing pain.
Missing pieces float beyond reach in empty space.
In cubist viewpoint, my world is fragmented.
Life continues. Nothing is the same.
Future dreams are cancelled by massive air strikes.
Carefully packed grocery bags rip beyond measure.
Parts of my life roll hopelessly away,
> down a large street choking with rush hour traffic.
Mates find new ways to fill the emptiness.
Mine will always remain a gaping hole.
Wounded, new skin grows over the abyss.
I know the missing part is out there somewhere.
Amputated, far removed beyond feeble grasp,
> my stump heals while I long for reconnection
> to a part that cannot be recovered.

March 17, 1999

I spent the beginning of my adult life trying not to be like my mother, trying to be a separate individual. What I learned through the years is that we carry a part of our parents with us always. I am now proud to be very much like my mother and understand that a part of me is gone. At the same time, I am also aware of my own uniqueness and differences. Part of her will always be with me.

How Could She?

How could she up and die, she so alive?
She left no farewell note, her things untouched,
    planned on getting well, living longer.
There was so much to live, yet
    I keep looking for signs of her alive.
None remain. She is gone.
A presence all my life, wanted or not,
    she lived through me, and so it continues.
We think mothers are here forever.
Only when they die do we see where we've been.
She died when so alive. How could she?
I become aware of my own mortality,
    clinging to her positive nature, discarding
    the negative.
Would she approve? I think so now.
We need to remember mothers for nurturing.
We become them ourselves.
How could she up and leave, for me to grieve?
Earthly parting, never easy, is not final.
Unfinished business will be complete in heaven.
There is still so much to live here and above.
Searching for my mother on earth,
    perhaps I look in wrong places.
Gone from my view, I hold her deep within.
A small pup sent wandering from the pack,
    I search my own life apart from the rest.
How can I do anything less?

March 17, 1999

Part of grieving involves anger for being abandoned. Grief opens a window on one's own mortality. We often think our parents will be around forever.

95

Three She Loves

In life she loved three more than all else.
Now she comes in spontaneous spirit visits,
            unexpected connections beyond mortal life.
Far she reaches with power not hers.
We see her in rainbows, in bright autumn leaves.
She meets us in dreams. Always she smiles.
Her effervescent happiness soothes our sorrow.
Three she loves, maintaining her connection.
Two daughters feel increased maternal warmth.
What of the man she shared half a century?
He's drowned sorrow in continuing, just living,
            missing little things, her smile,
            her unending energy.
Even her nagging would break unwelcome silence.
He wakes hours before dawn, unable to sleep.
Could it be she who tries connecting with him?

March 25, 1999

Both my sister and I felt our mother's love beyond the grave, like nothing we felt before. We also had visions of some kind in which we felt her presence. I wondered if my mother might be trying to connect with my father as well.

96

Five Months Enough

They weren't enough,
    those five cruel months.
No time for dying
    when life was rich.
Five months not enough,
    we sought recovery, not death.
Six months later,
    an eternity of grief,
    we sort through belongings,
    feeling empty.
Why did she not spare us
    dispersing her trappings?
Things used by mortals
    not needed beyond.
Will living continue,
    ever be again sane?
Five months not enough.
Lost in my misery,
    searching her things,
    failing to find,
    I overlooked her
    right in my heart.

March 28, 1999

I do not think we can ever be prepared to see a loved one die. Five months' warning was not enough, especially since my mother thought she was going to live. Or, did she just want to spare us?

Only One Missing

Am I the only one missing her sweet presence?
Where are her soul mates mourning her absence?
Everyone is busy with life, living and doing.
Not so different than she who is gone.
Why is her absence devastating me to pieces?
I a daughter fully grown, separate, independent.
Only when she left did I recognize how deep the bond.
It is like none other. There is only one mother.
Sometimes she loved too much. Living got in the way.
She was not always sweet. I toss out bad memories.
Now her love is perfect, as she is from above.
Wading through my grief, I am only one of many
      missing her life intersecting with mine.

March 29, 1999

It seemed everyone in my family went on with their lives and I was the only one still grieving. After reading "Blood and Paper," my dad tried to comfort me with the continually optimistic "cheer-up" phrase that had gotten me through childhood. It did not work this time.

One Year Ago

Brightly shone the sun one year ago today.
Bathed in resurrection joy, Easter bunny fun,
    together in church and meal, we celebrated God's gift.
Funny, now I can't recall that Easter Day together.
How would we know it would be our last?
We shared freely, unaware of looming trials.
Six months later, I still struggle to emerge
    from grief's pillage and utter desolation.
Conquering clutter in my home, I find a card
    sent from you to your precious granddaughter.
Unaware of events between then and now,
    innocent card signed with Easter hope.
Found while cleaning up grief's despair,
    re-opened one year later, I am reminded of you--
    bright cheer, bubbly joy, living energy...
    blotting out your earthly faults.
How different life can be in one short year.
We are too busy living to think
    beyond our earthly existence.
Where will I be one year hence, ten, or more?
Your card and my clutter reminds me.
Nothing of earth remains the same forever.
Drained by grief, Easter joy fills my emptiness.
In unexpected ways I am renewed.
Clear shines the sun again upon this new day,
    radiant reminder of hope in God's son,
    sent by you, in a card, one year ago.

April 12, 1999

Cleaning up after spring break, I came upon an Easter card Mother sent, dated 4/12/98. I remember her mentioning how difficult it was to find an age appropriate "granddaughter" Easter card. How ironic to find the card exactly one year later.

Mother

I wear her clothes.
I drive her car.
I have her genes.
I feel her energy
   when mine does wane.

I wear her watch upon my wrist.
I don her mother's ring.
I use her mirror.
I see the same eyes,
   though mine are brown.

I think like her.
I walk like her.
I almost feel I am her.
I hear her voice come from my mouth,
   but look in the mirror and still find me.

      April 27, 1999

Graduation
Joanne in 1947 and Debbie on April 30, 1999.

I promised Mother I would walk across the stage of Hill Auditorium to receive my degree from the University of Michigan. To my surprise, her oncologist was one of the speakers at the ceremony. This was the man who visited her deathbed saying, "Relax and let go." I also needed to follow his advice and let go of my loss in order to appreciate my own achievement. As the Men's Glee Club sang from the balcony, it sounded as if a heavenly host was filling the auditorium.

Life Hug

Trapped in disease warped body,
     you wanted life.
Fresh mind caught in war-zone,
     you wanted peace.
Time bomb hidden deep within,
     detonated, ready to blow,
     you were helpless.
Life choices gave you time to savor,
     you continued living.
Time to feel, smell and hug,
     you fought hard.
While your body slowly succumbed,
     you went within.
People cared and ministered,
     you felt humbled.
They sent food, flowers and cards,
     you felt loved.
Cancer ravaged your body,
     you moved beyond.
No longer impeded by this world,
     you gained true life.
Life memories linger amid the ruins,
     we feel your peace.
Remembered life-hugs reconnect,
     your life circles my heart.

May 1, 1999

Written a year to the day of Mother's colon surgery, I still feel her life hugs while I continue living. Her essence lingers in my father's garden.

April 30, 1998
I suggested we take photos as mother
was leaving for the hospital.

Caretaker Claude

Caretaker Claude kept peace in the home
     gentle and kind as a boy then a man.
He formed quite a team with the woman he married.
She was his sparkle, his voice, and his queen.
They had lots of friends in town and afar,
     in home or at restaurant, always most gracious.
Traveling in groups or alone they did all.
He was Prince Valiant for fifty plus years.

Caretaker Claude was nurse to his mate.
Fueled by loving devotion
     he came at a whistle
     whenever he heard it.
Fresh flowers from his garden
     he arranged for the table.
You name it he did it,
     cooking, washing, bathing, nursing.
He drove and he carried.
He gave shots and warm caresses.
Proud of his home pharmacy,
     he ordered and doled medications.
He stoically accepted whatever occurred,
     took care of each need, except for his own.

Caretaker Claude left alone he did grieve.
His voice became a new tool,
     always there but unheard until now.
He remembered and tried to keep on with his life,
     resuming those things he once did with his wife.
Continuing on he must do as they did,
     filling the void in his single new life.

                     May 7, 1999

Joanne and Claude, 1944

. . . . and 1998.

"Caretaker Claude" was conceived as I watched my father devotedly care for Mother during her illness. He was able to keep her at home for all but twenty-one hours. A hospice nurse visited weekly during the summer, but stopped coming because Mother was doing so well. Until her final week. Hospice residence gave our family the opportunity to concentrate on the situation, enabling us precious final hours. I do not know of any man who would have done more than my father did for his dying wife.

Spring Testimony

I mourn too long the death of spring.
Long since its passing, grieving my loss
       whether I like it or not, it comes--
       brightly returning to my withered soul.
Warm sun soothes my skin.
Trees burst in effulgent bloom.
Rebirth cannot be ignored.
Each perfect petal blooms for a spell,
       magenta, white, pink, deep purple,
       caught in wind changes
       swirling through my life.
As they fade to pale colors,
       millions are freed from each tree.
Spent blossoms fall as snow to the ground,
       a confetti celebration no longer needed.
Who sweeps up from nature's festivity?
No need to be tidy. It all blows away,
       some to the earth, some in the air,
       swiftly filling in forgotten places.
Fragile spring petals appeal to my heart,
       spring testimony to the cycle of life.
I walk amid a floating canopy of blossoms.
Beauty surrounds and fills my emptiness.
My heart sheds spent grief petals
       scattered beyond reach. I must let them go.
                     May 7, 1999

Seven months have passed, and my loss is just as great. Nothing replaces a mother. There are still moments of unbelief that this happened. Someone once told me that grief never goes away completely. I am learning to live with it. The depth of my grief tells me the depth of our bond. What better testimony could I offer? My mother will always live on in me.

Grandma's Car

Unexpected gifts are always the best.
You've waited for this time to drive.
I watch you leave before my eyes.
How did sixteen come so soon?
Here you are in grandma's car.
She always drove neat white wheels.
One year ago they were hers.
Today we celebrate a milestone,
    sweet sixteen, bittersweet your acquisition.
May you feel grandma's wings driving,
    protecting, guiding along your life-road.

May 9, 1999

This poetic grief journey ends as it began, with a birthday poem. We are all changed by grief. It manifests itself in many different ways in each one of us. A year has passed since the cancer appeared. My grief remains. Perhaps the journey never ends. We have but a while to walk together in person but an eternity to walk together in spirit.

My Daughter

My daughter
A gift from God
My rock
Precious jewel with many facets-
Deep thinker - thoughts divine
Creator of
     music, art, written words,
     life, emotions, love, human depth,
Faces adversity with strength and Christian love.
Bent like the twig
Bounces back, braver, stronger
Priceless jewel -
     undeserving me.

Joanne Rebeck

As far as I know, this is the only poem Mother ever wrote for me. Written on a scrap of paper stuffed in her address book, I found it a year and a half after she died. Why she never gave it to me I'll never know. This gift means so much that I decided to let her voice be my conclusion to Riding Past Grief.

Index

Illustration credits:

> *Betsy Ash: front cover; 1, 31, 43, 49, 50, 53, 62*
> *Deborah Ash: 7, 68*
> *Jeffrey Ash: 79*
> *Mark Ash: 32, 34, 41, 70*

Bottom photo on page 16 copyright *Plymouth-Canton Community Crier.*
Photos on page 45 by Edgar Westrum.
Back cover photo by Don P. Proctor